By Siblings, For Siblings

siblings of people with disabilities supporting
other siblings of people with disabilities

NATALIE HAMPTON & NICOLE HAMPTON

Illustrated by NICOLE HAMPTON

dedicated to our brother Jake

If you are a sibling of a person with a disability, we wrote this book for you. But while we are writing to you specifically, we hope that this book may also help others — whether they be parents, caretakers, other relatives, or friends. We hope that everyone reading this book will come away having learned more about the experiences and emotions of siblings of people with disabilities.

Table of Contents

Introduction

Our older brother Jake had MPS II, also known as Hunter syndrome. It was a mental and physical disability, and by the time he passed away in 2019 at the age of 17, he hadn't walked or talked in years.

Over one billion people in the world have some form of disability, about one-fifth of which are serious.[1] Many of them have at least one sibling. Jake had us.

Our experiences as Jake's sisters are core to our identities and lives. An important part of our experiences was connecting with other siblings of people with disabilities. We were fortunate to participate with Jake in many organizations that helped children with disabilities. Some of the organizations were Friday night groups; others were summer camps. At all of them, what made us different in the broader world allowed us to fit right in at these programs.

During these programs, we connected with other siblings who could relate to our experiences; many of them have stayed close friends since. Although we don't remember it, our mom tells us a story from when we were younger that highlights just how important these connections were to us. We told a friend that our brother, who tried to chew everything within reach, once picked up our dog's leg and bit it. Even our dog was shocked. But our friend wasn't, and she even one-upped us with a story of what her own autistic brother recently did. If we had told this to another friend, they might have been disgusted or weirded out by our brother. But because we each had the shared

1 The World Bank, 2021

---

experience of being siblings of someone with a disability, it felt normal and we continued on our conversation without pausing.

It's these types of connections that are incredibly important and valuable to siblings of people with disabilities. We're lucky to have each other, so we've never felt completely alone. Many other kids don't have this same built-in support system, so it's important for them to reach out to and connect with other siblings of people with disabilities.

In summer 2021, with the COVID-19 pandemic still raging, many people (including us) felt isolated and disconnected from the rest of the world. We started thinking of ways we could help people reconnect, particularly siblings of people with disabilities. Out of that, Special Siblings Connect was born. It's dedicated to helping support these siblings, foster connections between them, and create awareness for them. Our first major project is *By Siblings, For Siblings*.

In this book we aren't trying to replace medical advice or research, and it isn't meant to be a how-to guide. We know from experience that there is no one pre-set way to be a sibling. Rather, we are offering our own and others' experiences and stories as siblings. They are meant to show other siblings of people with disabilities that they aren't alone, and that many other people can relate to their experiences and emotions. We hope these stories will resonate with and help readers.

How is the book organized?

After collecting quotes, advice, and stories, we noticed that a few emotions appeared to be common. We divided this book into five of them based on our personal experience and what we learned. These emotions aren't black and white — they frequently overlap, and stories often contain aspects of multiple emotions. Each section begins with an introduction to the emotion and how it might apply specifically to siblings of people with disabilities. Next, the sections contain quotes, advice, and longer stories by siblings, for siblings.

We begin first with four emotions that are typically considered negative: siblings of people with disabilities often feel different, isolated, embarrassed, and sorrow. We want to show that these emotions are completely valid, and that other siblings aren't alone in experiencing them. Some of the pieces offer advice on how to deal with the emotions; others just provide solidarity.

The fifth emotion is gratitude. While it often can be challenging to recognize positive emotions, they are still there. Since positive emotions like gratitude may not feel as intense as negative ones, it's easy to spend less time reflecting on them. But we thought it was important to focus on how much gratitude someone can feel as a sibling of someone with a disability, and these pieces really highlight that gratitude. We hope this section especially can bring new light to other siblings' perspectives.

These five emotions do not nearly cover the entire spectrum of emotions that these siblings feel. The reader may notice some notable ones, such as love, missing. Love is a strong and constant undercurrent in many of the other emotions we discuss. Siblings of people with disabilities feel a tremendous amount of love for their sibling, but there is also an equally important need to express the hardships and feelings that those siblings face. This book attempts to do that.

At the end, we list other resources to explore. These include other organizations and books. Though we hope Special Siblings Connect and *By Siblings, For Siblings* help support siblings of people with disabilities, we know it is important to connect in many ways, and we urge people to look into these resources.

After each quote and story, we provide a first name and the condition of the sibling. We chose not to define the conditions. Based on our own experience, we've noticed that every condition manifests differently and experiences from one condition can easily apply to many others. Also, knowledge on conditions can change over time. For these reasons, we decided not to define the conditions. If interested, there are plenty of resources online to provide a more in-depth look at them.

Final Notes:

In the process of writing this, we contacted over a hundred organizations for people with disabilities and their siblings. The following quotes, advice, and stories are from those who responded. By no means are they meant to represent everyone. Although they may have many things in common, they are all unique — as every story and situation is. If you would like to share your unique story as a sibling of someone with a disability, go to specialsiblingsconnect.org/join to submit it for blog posts and for other future projects.

This book is meant to connect and not be divisive. Also, certain acceptable terminology can change over time and certain terminology that is considered offensive to one person is considered the correct terminology for others. In particular, terms such as "disabled," "special needs," "different," "atypical," and "differently abled" are debated, and we have heard recommendations both for and against each term. Out of respect for those courageous enough to share their stories, we kept the terminology they used as this book is supposed to support and not judge. Based on feedback we have heard, we have chosen to use the term disabled, but this isn't to imply that people with disabilities don't have strengths and talents.

We really hope these stories can help you. Thank you for reading.

Best,
Natalie Hampton & Nicole Hampton
Founders, Special Siblings Connect
Houston, Texas

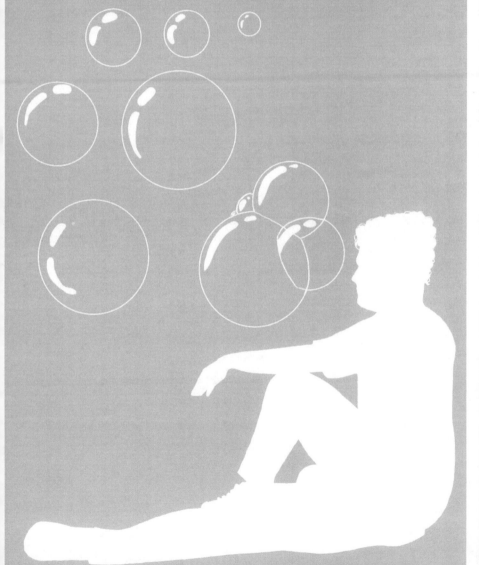

DIFFERENT

Introduction to Different

What does it mean to be different? The notion of "different" is rooted in comparisons, either to a specific thing or to the perceived "regular" world. If you — a sibling of someone with a disability — compare your family to other families without disabilities, you will inevitably notice lots of differences. What is normal to families with disabilities is hardly normal to families without, and vice versa.

And within these families with disabilities, no two are alike. The same can be said about families without disabilities: there are always differences from family to family. That's the problem with feeling different: no matter what you do, you will never be exactly the same as someone else.

You may feel that because your sibling is different, you are different by association. In your head, this difference may feel bad. Once sucked into the cycle of noticing differences, it can feel impossible to escape. You could be hyperaware of every way your life veers away from your perception of what is traditional. You may hate being called different and hate the reminder of all those differences.

Based on our experiences, we realized that being different isn't a bad thing. Instead of shying away from the unusual and unique aspects of our lives, we learned to embrace them. We discovered that there is no universal definition of what is normal: it is all about our perspective.

In this section, the siblings of someone with a disability discuss moments when they either felt different or felt like their sibling was different. Some of the quotes show you that you are not alone in these feelings. Some of the quotes show how the siblings reframed these differences as a positive for which they are now thankful.

Quotes, Advice, and Stories

❝ Everyone always tells me, "Oh that must have been so hard growing up with your brother," but it's all I've ever known, so then it makes me feel like I've missed out on something else. You haven't; it's just a different perspective of life. Every family has their own lessons and hardships and joys. Sharing experiences with others really helps to lessen the gap. ❞

JESSICA
Sibling's condition: Cerebral palsy

❝ When people stared at my brother in public, I always felt like they were staring right at me and judging me. I was both mad at them for their looks and wanted to hide from them. I wanted to defend my brother, but I also wanted to defend myself. ❞

NATALIE
Sibling's condition: Hunter syndrome

❝ At a young age, I learned to not compare my family with other families because we ultimately have a purpose/journey that is very special. ❞

LYDIA
Sibling's condition: Autism (PDD-NOS)

❝ It is hard not having a sibling that I can play and interact with more like my friends' siblings. I wish Clara could do more with me (like play Barbies or dolls). But I try to just have as much fun with her as I can. I try to make her laugh by singing silly songs and hanging out in her room after dinner even if she isn't paying attention. I try to make her smile even if she won't ever interact like I hope. ❞

CAMILLE
Sibling's condition: Cohen Syndrome

❝ I wish I could do daily things with my sister. I wish I could go to school with her, go shopping with her, go on car rides with her, take pictures with her. All these things that normal kids take for granted, I would do anything to have with my sister. I wake up every day hoping she's awake too. Every night I go to bed and pray she wakes up and doesn't die because of a seizure in her sleep. It's hard to do anything with her. She can't go to stores, she can't go to regular schools, she can't go to the movies, she can't hangout with people, and she can't do anything a normal person can. I just want to have a single family dinner with her there where she's not having a seizure or misbehaving. I would love to hang out with my sister like normal siblings do, but I can't because she's either sleeping because of her seizures or misbehaving. I remember one time we were trying to take a walk with our family, and she fell to the floor and had one of the worst seizures. 911 was called, and it was scary for everyone. I just wish I could live life with my sister without worrying 24/7 if she's going to make it. ❞

SAMANTHA
Sibling's condition: Dravet syndrome

❝ It's hard seeing other people say, "Let's go to the YMCA," and 2 minutes later they are driving there. For my family, we have to decide that an hour beforehand and decide who stays home with my sister. Then half an hour later, something happens so that we end up leaving at least an hour later than planned. ❞

NOVELLE
Sibling's condition: Cerebral palsy

❝ There are times when I feel left out or like we are not doing things as a family as we previously did before my brother came... but we have worked out our own ways of fun that give him his sensory needs and keep him happy: pillow fights, walks in parks, and dancing with music make up for the fun missed by going out. ❞

JAI
Sibling's condition: Autism

❝ It is strange to live in a house where one can just adjust, pick up and get things done. My brother requires a routine and hates change. When new things come up, there is always a bit of hesitation because we don't know how he will react. I hate how people at birthday parties stare at him. It's okay that he is overstimulated. Not everyone handles changes the same way. I'm glad to know that I can be there to remove such stares. I have a great back-off look. ❞

GABI
Sibling's condition: ODD, ADHD,
Cerebral dysrhythmia, on the Autism spectrum

❝ Having a sibling with special needs provides you with a unique opportunity to develop a different perspective on life. Johnny has broadened my perspective in life in major ways and has given me the ability to look at things at different angles. It's our job as siblings of those with special needs to capitalize on that opportunity and use our perspective to make the lives of our siblings, ourselves, and those around us better. ❞

VINCE
Sibling's condition: Autism

❝ Know there are other siblings like you going through the same things. ❞

LIZ
Sibling's condition: Chromosome 2 disorder,
heart condition, visual and hearing impairment

❝ Everyone in the family behaves according to his or her perspective towards the situation. Try to be a little open to everyone's understanding. ❞

JAI
Sibling's condition: Autism

❝ My sister is physically disabled, and she does not get to do sports. One thing she likes to do is throw me baseball pitches because she wants to play sports like me. I always stop what I'm doing and let her throw pitches to me no matter what. I do this because I know she needs kindness and special attention and I know that a small act goes a long way for her. ❞

ELLIOT
Sibling's condition: Down syndrome

❝ Where is Conner?" The movie ended, but my brother, Conner, was nowhere to be found. In a matter of seconds, my brother disappeared from my grandmother's care and panic set in. Complete strangers from across the movie theater joined my family's search. The theater went into lockdown as security searched the building. Meanwhile, my mom, grandma, and I looked in each theater. Six theaters down, there he was — totally unaware of the chaos around. I felt the biggest sigh of relief at the sight of a short, stubby boy appearing in the distance. Standing at the edge of the first row, my brother was crunching on the buttered popcorn of a total stranger. In a nutshell, that was Conner. He was here one moment, and then mysteriously gone the next. Yet, no matter where he went, he somehow was and is always with me.

Where is Conner? That really could be the refrain of my life. When he was alive, he might wander off, but we would always find him. I would give anything to just be looking for him in a restaurant — where I might find him eating french fries off a stranger's plate. But the reason my brother would do this puzzling and sometimes amusing thing is that he had a disease that would ultimately take his life when he was 15.

My brother is still my brother. And my brother is no longer alive, and I am not an only child. I am, in fact, the only child living in my household. In 6th grade, I came to Emery, pretty much not knowing anyone. In 6th grade, I was navigating a new school and new people on my own. Those that knew me in sixth grade knew that I was Jamie, the girl that wore big bows in my hair, while only some may have realized that I had an older brother named Conner, and that he had a disability because his disease made that obvious. Conner was born with a disease called Mucopolysaccharidosis II, also known as Hunter Syndrome, a genetic disease that only affects boys. The progression of this horrific disease ultimately leads to an inability to talk, walk, and eat, and eventually death.

I always knew that one day I would be an "only" child, but in the months before Conner died, I was consumed with the excitement of starting a new chapter in my life, 6th grade, which started off great! I started Emery literally with bows in my hair (that did not last long!) and I made friends quickly. I felt like I belonged. But then Thanksgiving came. Conner had been stable for a long time. But the day after Thanksgiving, Conner began having seizures, and by Sunday, he was gone. I left for Thanksgiving break as the younger sibling of Conner. I came back to school without him. He was just three weeks away from his big 16th birthday. I dreaded returning to school after his passing, but my school community showed me enormous support and kindness.

Conner was never what people would call "typical", but he was my "big" brother, and he was my hero from the earliest time I can remember. Conner was always around with a smile, a laugh, and a hug. What was life like for Conner? Conner needed 24-hour care. He had a feeding tube and slept in a hospital bed. He needed help to do everything. I often helped him. When home, I was in his room. I watched Drake and Josh with him and loved hearing him laugh. I picked up the toys he dropped or threw across the room like a game of catch. We went on walks; I pushed his wheelchair. We talked — actually I talked and he listened — and I tried to understand what he wanted and needed. Yes, this was different from what most have with siblings, but it was normal to me.

He was just my big brother and though I was four years younger in age, our roles reversed very early in our lives. Though Conner suffered immensely throughout his short life, he also experienced indescribable love, and he left me with lessons that have forever changed my life, perspective, and relationships. For him, I would do anything, and I took on the responsibility to help care for him, be with him, and ensure he always had a friend around him. For most people, siblings are the ones you might compete with or fight with. Oh, what I would give to have a sibling to fight with. Yes, this is a loss for me, but I don't regret what I had with Conner. It has made me who I am: a more compassionate, patient, and mature person. Ultimately, a person who truly values relationships enough that my friends have become the siblings I no longer have.

Where is Conner? Conner is still with me. His life was brief, but his impact is immense.

Losing Conner meant that I lost my best friend and my biggest inspiration. After he died it was challenging at times to watch my friends hug their siblings in the hall. When a teacher or a stranger asked if I had any siblings, I never knew when to say yes or when to say no. It is a constant struggle for me to decide when it's necessary to tell people that my brother passed away when they ask, because that always makes people uncomfortable. But I have a sense of guilt when I don't mention him to a stranger that asks because I am NOT an only child, and I never will be. My experience and time with him, without question, influenced me as a person. Without him, I would not be who I am today. Even though I am physically an only child, I will never claim to be one because those two words do not capture who I am and was as a sister — an essential part of my identity. Only child: those two words also make my brother's life seem irrelevant and relegating his life to irrelevance would be an atrocity. No one could ever replace him as my brother, friend, or hero and his impact on who I am is permanent and significant. I am not an only child, but I am a person whose sibling died very young, but that sibling continues to affect who I am and how I live my life.

One reason I am able to say I am not an only child is that my parents had the wisdom and the courage to allow me to be part of his life. Lots of siblings of special needs children do not have that opportunity. Their parents want to shield them from what can be an incredibly painful experience. I understand this and I am grateful my parents had the foresight to realize I needed to be part of my brother's life because he was my brother and no matter how painful his experience was, I was part of it and he was part of mine.

Conner faced immense suffering, yet never failed to stay positive and strong. Everything around him was failing, but he never stopped smiling. He prepared me for the good, bad and constant changes that we all face. I use his strength to process everything in my world. I try to solve issues or minor disputes quickly. I try to confront things that are important and brush off the trivial all because I know it's really insignificant compared to the big stuff. No matter how challenging my circumstances may be, I know that my brother persevered through much more demanding conditions. He kept going — fighting and believing. Instead of "losing Conner," I made a choice to bring him with me by taking advantage of every opportunity he never got to experience.

As my next chapter begins, I will carry forward the lessons Conner taught me. He was much more than what was seen on the surface — a little boy with an enlarged head sitting silently in a wheelchair. Yes, he looked and acted differently. But, to me he was "normal." The daily stares from children never fazed me, yet the ones from adults angered me. I now understand that while Conner was different, we are all different. Conner taught me the importance of accepting others no matter the label that society attaches to them. He taught me to embrace and not to judge and work to accept others for who they are — no matter who they are — or what their life circumstances may be. He changed me, and I hope to change others, especially those with special needs. I still get asked, "Where is Conner?" And, my answer is always the same: "Where he will always be, with me, wherever I go.*"*

JAMIE
Sibling's condition: Hunter syndrome

❝ In the book *The Curious Incident of the Dog in the Night-Time*, it is never explicitly stated that Christopher is autistic. It's just an unspoken assumption, scraped together from his habits and thoughts. Inevitably, everyone hops on that conjecture, even if they were trying not to be presumptuous.

When my English class discussed this book, people were so scared to use the word "autism" in our discussions. Until my teacher said that we could assume him to be autistic, everyone just said he was "different." The same people that argue against using "autistic" as an insult were essentially doing the same thing by treating the word as taboo. They weren't scared to theorize about who killed the dog (the mystery of the novel), but they wouldn't put the reasonable conclusion they reached into words until someone else had done so.

Still, everyone in the class, including the teacher, seemed scared of saying something offensive. When someone used the word "disabled" in reference to Christopher, my teacher corrected them, saying the correct term was "differently abled."

Differently abled.

Everyone is "differently abled," as in they are able to do different things. So, sure, it wasn't incorrect, but it doesn't replace "disabled." Disabled isn't an incorrect term. There are things that Christopher couldn't do because his mind wouldn't let him. By definition, he was disabled. Refusing to use the term "disabled" invalidates this fact.

And I was the only one in the class who had a problem with the teacher's solution of "differently abled." Maybe calling Christopher "differently abled" made some people feel better, appeasing their sense of guilt for thinking he was disabled. They couldn't see anything wrong with the term and they couldn't understand why I was so bothered by it.

I thought about what would have happened if someone called my brother "differently abled." My brother who had passed away months ago because of his disability. My brother couldn't walk or talk his last year; he could scarcely breathe or eat.

When I brought my class discussion up to my family, they had the same reaction as me. It was just factually false, trying to masquerade the fact that Christopher, biologically, couldn't do the same things as others. It's not that my class didn't have good intentions, trying to not insult him. But in refusing to say "disabled," they were turning a medical term into the insult they feared. Not only was the term discrediting my brother's experience, but mine and my whole family's that were so affected by his inability to do many things. My brother was disabled, and, sure, it made some things hard, but he was still the best brother and it didn't negate his worth and get rid of my never ending love and connection with him. Being disabled didn't make him inferior but rather allowed his strengths to shine. He knew every Disney song, was flexible, funny and giving, and could make anyone smile.

My brother has allowed me to see the world through a wider, more accepting lens. So maybe my embracing the terminology is something you can only understand if you are in this situation, related to someone with special needs. Then "disabled" isn't an insult, just an unequivocal reality pervading all aspects of life. 🙶

NICOLE
Sibling's condition: Hunter syndrome

🙶 The week after my brother passed away, teachers didn't know how to treat me. They left sticky notes on my desk that said *I'm so sorry for your loss*, they apologized in the halls, they wrote emails, they let me turn in my work late, they turned a blind eye if I was chewing gum in class, though technically against school policy. They couldn't understand why my sister and I were at school instead of at home with family. It wasn't because we were grieving less or didn't care, but we found comfort in the routine of school. We found comfort in seeing our friends and going to classes. (Advice #1: Everyone deals with their circumstances and situations differently, and just because you deal with it differently than someone else, that doesn't make your reaction any less valid. Find what makes you feel best.)

When we missed school for his funeral, my US history teacher had all the students sign a card for us, and while I'm very appreciative of it, it also highlighted to everyone that our brother died. We weren't just classmates anymore, but we were those girls with a dead brother. Previously in elementary school, a similar reputation had followed. It seemed like everyone knew our brother: he was always smiling, always laughing, always drawing people to him. And because of his physical disabilities, he was recognizable.

So for my entire life up until high school, I was known by virtue of him. But freshman year as I entered a new school with few people who had gone to my elementary or middle school, I had the opportunity to start over. When asked how many siblings I had, I could answer one sister with only a slight hesitation, and when there were days that were harder than others because I missed him, I could make up other reasons why. I could say it was just school stress or lack of sleep. (Advice #2: There will always be harder days. Take it day by day.)

I considered it at first — starting over and making sure I didn't acquire the same label — but to me, that felt like erasing him. Without him, I wouldn't be the person I am today, and it felt wrong to pretend so. I'm not shaming anyone who has faced a similar decision and chose differently, because everyone has different circumstances and there is no one clear answer. (Advice #3: Don't take any advice as prescriptive. It's about knowing your circumstances and your comforts and what feels right to you. What felt right to me might not be what feels right to everyone else.)

To me, the right answer was to continue to acknowledge him and his influence on me. It made for some awkward conversations when I brought him up for the first time and people didn't know how to react — and I never expected anyone to — but it still felt right. It also allowed me to connect to others who had similar experiences, whether it was losing someone close to them or having a disabled sibling themselves.

It gave me a support system of people I could talk to and who would listen, even if they didn't fully understand what I was going through. That network has been key to keeping me going in numerous ways. (Advice #4: Find that support system and know they are there for you. You will have emotions and feelings that are completely normal and valid and having people you can talk to about them is incredibly valuable.)

My entire life, I've had the label of the sibling of a disabled kid. When I was younger, I felt more unsure and scared of the title, but now, I realize it is something I should embrace, because yes — I am the sibling of a disabled kid, and I always will be, and it will always be a major part of my identity that I don't want to hide. 🙿

NATALIE
Sibling's condition: Hunter syndrome

ISOLATED

Introduction to Isolated

The Merriam-Webster Dictionary defines isolation as, "the state of being in a place or situation that is separate from others." Separation breeds loneliness.

For siblings of those with disabilities, isolation can be quite prominent. From personal experience, there are multiple potential causes. You feel different and separated from others. You may think that others don't understand disabilities and consequently don't understand you. These things could lead you to feel like you are all alone. We have certainly felt that way.

Similarly, you may feel like you cannot discuss your problems with others. You may think your feelings are invalid and unimportant. You may feel the need to be the perfect child to compensate for your sibling with a disability; you may not want to burden your parents or caretakers by discussing your own thoughts and problems. And you also may feel ignored, thinking (rightly or wrongly) that your sibling with a disability always gets more attention.

But you are never alone: you just might not realize that there is potential to gain strength from many sources around you.

In this section, we look at quotes by siblings of someone with a disability discussing moments they have felt isolated in their lives and how they dealt with those feelings. Many emphasize how important it has been to connect with others to combat these feelings of isolation.

Quotes, Advice, and Stories

❝ You may feel alone, but you are not alone in that feeling. ❞

NICOLE

Sibling's condition: Hunter syndrome

❝ Don't say you are fine just because you feel the family can't handle the extra burden. ❞

LIZ

Sibling's condition: Chromosome 2 disorder,
heart condition, visual and hearing impairment

❝ Finding some people to talk with is so important. Other siblings are the greatest resource for this, but even if you cannot connect with other siblings, find some friends who will support you. You are never alone, and it is important to have people surrounding you that remind you of this. ❞

NATALIE

Sibling's condition: Hunter's syndrome

❝ I wish I knew, growing up, anyone who knew what I was going through. Now I know there are a lot of people who can relate. I wouldn't have felt so alone. ❞

JESSICA

Sibling's condition: Cerebral palsy

❝ Our Dad died suddenly when I was 17, and 7 of the 8 of us siblings were living with our parents. My Dad did not have a will or life insurance, which was really tough for my mom. After that, my mom got a will and a trust, but it was not a special needs trust and ended up making my brothers ineligible for needed benefits. When our mom passed away, we knew nothing of the system and had never met any other sibs. We struggled and made many mistakes until we finally found SibNet and made some helpful connections. We were in our 40s when we finally got connected to other sibs and some support. It was so helpful. As our dear friend Don Meyer says, it should not take 40 plus years to find your peeps and support. ❞

NORA
Sibling's condition: Autism

❝ You are important. It's okay to want to be the center of attention sometimes. It's completely normal to have your own hopes and dreams centered only around yourself. ❞

LIZ
Sibling's condition: Chromosome 2 disorder,
heart condition, visual and hearing impairment

❝ I was often known as "Jake's sister." Although I loved my brother and was happy to be associated with him, I didn't understand why I was always "Jake's sister", and he wasn't "Natalie's brother." At school too, people knew him more than they knew me. He was distinct with his braces and constant wide smile, but I just wanted people to know and think about me too. ❞

NATALIE
Sibling's condition: Hunter syndrome

66 Most people are ignorant of the burdens and complexities of disabilities, but you understand those hardships more than most. Use that insight to find ways to help your sibling, your family, and families like yours. 99

NATHAN
Sibling's condition: Phelan-McDermid syndrome

66 If people ever give you crap for having a sibling with special needs, just know that you're not alone. Ignore them because they have no clue what your life is like. People are going to be rude, but never let it ruin you because you are a light to your sibling and so many others. 99

SAMANTHA
Sibling's condition: Dravet syndrome

66 Recognize that there are certain things that will be different about your life at home because you have a sibling with special needs; you may feel like your sibling is loved more, or that your needs are not being met. Accept this fact with a willingness for patience, a goal of better communication, and an open heart and it will all become easier in the end. 99

CLAIRE
Sibling's condition: Autism

66 When I was younger, I thought that my needs weren't as important as my sister's. After all, she needed help to do the most basic physical tasks, and I was more than capable of solving my own problems. I wish I asked for help when I really needed it. 99

DANA
Sibling's condition: Centronuclear myopathy

66 Growing up, I dreamed of meeting someone my age who had a sibling with a disability who could understand the roller coaster of life at home. You would think the population of San Diego could easily meet this request, but no one showed up in our circle. My brother is 5 years younger than I am and has Cerebral Palsy. He cannot do anything independently and requires 24-hour care. He does not communicate in the traditional sense of using words; however, our family understands him the majority of the time through eye movements, body movements, face scrunches, vocalizations, cries, laughter, and smiles. His smile is one of the most beautiful things about him. 99

JESSICA
Sibling's condition: Cerebral palsy

66 Sometimes I get sad that my parents have to constantly stop and help my sister when they are playing with me. 99

CAMILLE
Sibling's condition: Cohen Syndrome

66 Your needs matter. Speak up, ask for help, and advocate for yourself if you feel your needs are not being adequately taken care of. You are loved. 99

DANA
Sibling's condition: Centronuclear myopathy

66 Siblings need to connect with other siblings. It is so helpful and life-changing. 99

NORA
Sibling's condition: Autism

" Oftentimes, our siblings can't communicate through traditional means. Learning to understand your sibling is invaluable in communicating with others throughout the rest of your life. **"**

NATHAN
Sibling's condition: Phelan-McDermid syndrome

" Feeling isolated and lonely sucks. There is no way to sugarcoat it. But it's also not a permanent condition. Know that even if you feel isolated for a moment, you will ultimately end up getting out of that state (even if it is hard at the time). **"**

NATALIE
Sibling's condition: Hunter syndrome

" It's not weird to have a therapist; find someone else to confide in. **"**

LIZ
Sibling's condition: Chromosome 2 disorder,
heart condition, visual and hearing impairment

" Sometimes your sibling might take precedence. That doesn't mean you're not also important, but all kids have times where they need a little more attention. **"**

NICOLE
Sibling's condition: Hunter syndrome

" Life hasn't been easy for me and perhaps for you, but I am so thankful for all the good I get to experience with each day. This message encourages me along the way: "We can rejoice, too, when we run into problems and trials, for we know that they help us develop endurance. And endurance develops strength of character, and character strengthens our confident hope of salvation." —Romans 5.

As a sibling caregiver, I have experienced stress in managing the homework of caring for not only my sibling with disabilities but also other relatives while managing school and office work as an engineer, educator, and entrepreneur. I often don't immediately find time for myself. What has helped me has been growing a community of support with fellow sibling caregivers. We laugh, we cry, we celebrate, we mourn, we learn, we overcome together. We are reminded that we are not alone. And day by day, we become less lost navigating the complex wilderness of disability and care. 〞

If you're a sibling caregiver, check out AKALAKA, a community of support for gaining clarity, connection, and confidence on your journey, akalaka.org.

VICTORIA
Sibling's condition: Intellectual/Developmental Disability

❝ You don't have to be perfect. 〞

LIZ
Sibling's condition: Chromosome 2 disorder,
heart condition, visual and hearing impairment

❝ Sometimes siblings feel invisible. My sister's medical needs were often scary, complex, and unpredictable. I often felt invisible growing up as doctors, occupational therapists, speech therapists, and my sister's many other specialists paid attention to her needs and the needs of my parents. I was the forgotten sibling, or sometimes simply known as "(sister's) sibling" who spent every weekend dragged around from appointment to appointment. I want you to know that you have an identity. Yes, you are a sibling, and that job is often challenging and sometimes even rewarding, but your individuality matters. Your interests and talents matter. Your ability to feel a connection with your sibling matters. If you're able to communicate with your sibling and family unit, please do what I didn't know how to do and talk about it if you're feeling invisible. Encourage them to spend time with you. Encourage special jobs or tasks that will help build your confidence and self-worth. **"**

DANA
Sibling's condition: Centronuclear myopathy

" Find other siblings! So important — even if you don't talk about anything sibling or disability related, just knowing that you can be fully honest and real with them and they will understand is so freeing. **"**

NATALIE
Sibling's condition: Hunter syndrome

" I hate Thanksgiving. Let me correct myself. I love the food and the family time; however, it's what comes after I hate. The posting of "perfect" families with "perfect" siblings is what gets me. And I know nobody's perfect, and every family has its flaws; it just doesn't feel like that.

Eli has autism, which has made it hard for me to feel like one of those "Instagram families." This was hard for me when I was younger because I just couldn't understand why someone who looked like me acted so different and needed more attention. It was hard for me to accept that Eli cannot change who Eli is and that is okay.

He has always been an active kid. He learned to ride a bike at a young age, and now it's his favorite thing to do. Everyone in my neighborhood knows Eli, either as "Eli" or "The Biker Boy." Eli doesn't understand boundaries, so it wouldn't be unusual to find him walking into a neighbor's open garage or front door. It took me no time to realize that I would soon know everyone in my neighborhood because of Eli. He's even a "celebrity." Sometimes I'll be at school and people will come up to me (whom I've never spoken to) and say, "I didn't realize that kid was your brother. He's in my front yard all the time." Ah, typical Eli.

It's sometimes all we talk about in my house. Where is Eli? Is Eli ok? Has Eli taken his meds? My parents are always worried about Eli. It's a constant whirlwind of never-ending conversations where sometimes I feel like I can't tell my parents what I need or how I feel. When told there's a child with special needs in a family, no one first asks, "Well, how are his/her siblings handling it?"

Well, if you ask me, it feels like I'm alone, like no one around me gets it. I feel overlooked and expected more of. Often, I feel pressure to be "good" or "perfect" to make life easier for my parents. I get jealous and mad at my friends for having neurotypical siblings because they have never had to experience and never had to go through what I have been through. Sometimes, I just have so much anger that I get so upset because there is no one to put the blame on. I struggle, but I don't want people to know that, especially my parents.

It's difficult for me to open up because I've never had the opportunity to do so. It's hard for me to talk about because I know when I tell my friends, they won't really get it, but they'll nod their heads and tell me that it's going to be okay. But whatever emotions I am feeling on any day, I am extremely thankful for Eli.

Eli has made me, as a person, immensely strong. He doesn't even know it, but I am a better person with him. I am tough, I am resilient, I am understanding, I am determined, and most of all, I am thankful. It took me a long time to realize this, but I am so incredibly grateful that Eli is my brother, and I wouldn't change a thing about him.

So if there's anything I've realized, it's that these Thanksgivings are worth it. 🙶

BLYTHE
Sibling's condition: Autism

❝ The worst part of Colin's disability is his epilepsy. I can tell when he is having a seizure because I will hear a lot of running in the hall past my door. I can also tell that it stresses my parents, and that stresses me. The seizures make life unpredictable because they can happen at any time, anywhere. Colin can get hurt by falling down or convulsing. Foam usually comes out of his mouth, and sometimes he throws up. After it is over, everyone is drained and sort of in shock. It is horrible to watch, but I think my experiences with my brother have made me more empathetic to individuals with serious medical conditions. It also has made me realize how lucky I am to have good health.

Why am I sharing all this? It is not to shock whoever is reading this or to parade my life in front of them like some circus performance for them to gawk and stare at. In many ways, it is difficult to talk about how Colin's experience has affected me personally. On one hand, it obviously has affected my life. On the other hand, I am not the one living with special needs. I do not want to make Colin's experience all about me. If I am describing what living with Colin is like, I am doing it for just that: to describe it, to inform, to attempt to span what in many ways is an unbridgeable divide.

Most people do not understand what it is like to live with someone with special needs. Some people obliviously ignore handicapped individuals as if they are invisible, while others stare stupidly at them in public. Going to the grocery store with Colin can be challenging. People often stare at Colin because he may be loud or violate their personal space. This is a time when I would prefer oblivious ignoring. When I see families with special needs children in public, I make a conscious effort not to appear concerned or surprised. That way, they do not feel the discomfort I feel in those situations. Fortunately for Colin, he spends most days sheltered from a world that is unsure how to relate to him. Colin is lucky to attend an autism school where he is amongst equally special peers, and because he is so good-natured, he is the class favorite of both other students and teachers.

At home, life with Colin is somewhat uneventful, as long as I do not have visitors over. When I was younger, girls who would come over for playdates would sometimes complain about Colin being loud and ask, "Why is he so loud? Can you get him to stop?" Colin often vocalizes when he is engaging in stimming, self-stimulating behavior which includes repetition of movements and sounds. Also confusing to visitors, Colin does not understand property ownership, and once, he snatched a freshly baked cookie right out of my friend's hand. I did sympathize with her because she looked so shocked, but I thought she should be more understanding because this behavior is part of his disability. I generally feel that I am negatively judged by others for having a handicapped brother, but I refuse to be embarrassed. My love and respect for Colin are my shields, and it is my responsibility to show others how he should be treated. 🙶

KYRA
Sibling's condition: Autism

EMBARRASSED

.

Introduction to Embarrassed

Feeling embarrassed is hard to admit: as a sibling of someone with a disability you may love your sibling and know their disability isn't their fault, yet you sometimes want to hide from them in public. It's almost worse that it isn't their fault — even though they can not change their behavior, you desperately want your sibling to stop, and that might make you feel guilty.

For us and others, embarrassment was often accompanied by other emotions like anger and resentment. You might be angry at your sibling for interfering with your plans. You might resent your siblings for what they do — and what they cannot do.

These emotions might be difficult to admit to yourself; they can also be difficult to admit to others. When we felt embarrassed about our brother, we also felt great guilt and shame for feeling that way. We didn't want anyone else to know what negative emotions lay inside us. We especially didn't want to open up to our parents. We thought that we shouldn't be feeling how we did — because of that, we sometimes felt very alone.

In this section, siblings of someone with a disability discuss times they were embarrassed or angry. They also offer ways they dealt with these emotions. If you are experiencing these feelings you aren't alone, and many other siblings understand them.

Quotes, Advice, and Stories

❝ It's okay to feel times of resentment, frustration, or embarrassment. It doesn't mean you don't love your sib, and maybe they feel the same way about you. ❞

LIZ
Sibling's condition: Chromosome 2 disorder,
heart condition, visual and hearing impairment

❝ Put yourself in his/her shoes. Imagine how hard it would be to be like her and not be able to itch a scratch or tell someone what's wrong. ❞

NOVELLE
Sibling's condition: Cerebral palsy

❝ Being an older or younger sibling is a hard task on its own. Having a sibling with disabilities or special needs is another thing as well. Patience is required in this position as well as unconditional love. When you show your support for your sibling's accomplishments no matter how big or small they are, they feel proud of themselves. ❞

GABI
Sibling's condition: ODD, ADHD,
Cerebral dysrhythmia, on the Autism spectrum

“ Growing up, I myself had OCD (obsessive compulsive disorder) regarding the environments around me. This had to be there, and all of these had to be on that, and no one else could ruin how I had meticulously organized the spaces around me, or I would throw a tantrum. It got to the point of having anxiety when I felt that my organization was being threatened. This did not pair well at all with my brother who, with no concept of personal space nor full understanding of the fact that not everything belonged to him, would often times come into my room. He would throw my stuffed animals, go through my books to read them, and then leave all my stuff strewn across my room. I would scream, I would cry, and I would struggle with accepting that, at the time, my brother was still developmentally not in a position where he could understand when I said, "These are my things, don't touch them!" Nevertheless, my mother was able to teach me that, sometimes, sacrifices would have to be made for my brother. She did a great job meeting both of our needs, but it ultimately came down to me accepting my brother with open arms. I soon learned that my love for my brother went beyond the material aspects of my life. I grew patient and compassionate, two traits which have positively spread into many other parts of my life. My brother slowly began to improve on things like interacting with others and using his words to communicate his needs. I was able to express my boundaries in a way that helped both of us understand what the other sibling needed. My brother has always been someone I have loved but being able to iron out the wrinkles within our relationship over the past few years has not only improved both of us as individuals but has also strengthened our relationship and allowed our love for each other to run even deeper than it had before. ”

CLAIRE
Sibling's condition: Autism

❝ My brother's disability used to embarrass me, but now he is my biggest source of pride in life. ❞

NATHAN
Sibling's condition: Phelan-McDermid syndrome

❝ I love my brother and forever will. We have good and bad days. His medication helps him communicate and function. There are certain instances of anger that I do not appreciate that happen because of his ODD. But a person's actions are different then who they are. Life can get to be too overstimulating for him at times. But that is when the older sibling swoops in and saves the day. I have learned many things that help him calm down. ❞

GABI
Sibling's condition: ODD, ADHD,
Cerebral dysrhythmia, on the Autism spectrum

❝ One time we decided to go out to eat. My sister has to have specially formed seating for her wheelchair otherwise she is uncomfortable. Due to foam shortages, she was sitting in a seat that was WAY too small for her, but we had no way to get her a new one. As we were eating, she had a massive pain breakout because of how much pain she was in. We had to leave halfway through our meal because of this. It is hard living with a quadriplegic, non-verbal, spastic sister. Although I love her to bits, it can be pretty embarrassing and annoying sometimes. ❞

NOVELLE
Sibling's condition: Cerebral palsy

❝ As a young child, I often felt resentment about my brother's intellectual disability and embarrassment about his differences. Every aspect of my life was impacted by his challenges, and for many years, all I considered was how it affected me. I was frustrated by his vocalizations in public places. I wanted to distance myself from the kid who wore a lacrosse helmet around our school to protect his face from drop seizures. While I knew that my brother didn't have anyone else to stand up for him and that he didn't deserve the premature judgments that others made about him, I couldn't quite reconcile my negative feelings with the person I wanted to be. I think it's common for children to have a lot of different feelings about having a sibling with a disability. Unpacking my own feelings of embarrassment and then shame about my selfishness let me see my brother in a new light. The way he faces hardships has made him the most resilient role model in my life. The differences I once resented, like his high-energy and adventurous spirit, I've come to proudly embrace. My brother has taught me to appreciate the unique backgrounds, experiences, and hardships that individualize us. ❞

NATHAN
Sibling's condition: Phelan-McDermid syndrome

❝ My sister's behavior makes it so that I can never have people over at my house. This is not that much of a problem for me: I go out to see friends and do spend most of my time away from home. But my mom tells me that it feels like I'm never home and like I'm embarrassed of my sibling. I am not at all embarrassed of my sister, but I can tell that my mom truly believes that and it hurts her, but if I am going to have any friends at all, I have to spend all of my social time away from my house. To try to come to a compromise, I have little "play dates" with my sister when I have free time. We do puzzles, crafts, or watch television together, and then I can spend all of my other social time out of the house. Talking with my mom about how I felt while understanding where she was coming from allowed us to come to an agreement and keep everyone happy. **"**

EMMA
Sibling's condition: Dravet Syndrome

" My brother has manic episodes in which his anger escalates to a point in which he cannot control it. There was a time in which he wanted to wear a certain outfit to school but had spilled a drink on it. This all happened as we were supposed to head out the door. My brother could not handle the sensory overload of wet clothes and proceeded to wait for his clothes to finish from the dryer. My mother offered him another clean outfit, but change is hard and he was hyper fixated on that specific outfit. By that time, I was already late to school, so we convinced him to get in the car and drop me off, and by the time they came home, his pants would be dry. It was fine until we had been driving for about 5 minutes, and he completely lost it and threw a big fit. He was dysregulated and was crying. He then proceeded to be aggressive along with other things, but my mom and I stayed calm knowing that he simply needed time. Eventually, he calmed down when I began to tell him a story about gingerbread. By the time we got to my school, I was 30 minutes late and got a tardy. But that did not matter: he was calm and regulated again, which was the priority. **"**

GABI
Sibling's condition: ODD, ADHD,
Cerebral dysrhythmia, on the Autism spectrum

" At school, when I saw my brother in the halls, I was excited to see him and say hi — but I sometimes felt a bit embarrassed when it was obvious that he was having a bad day. I hated that I felt embarrassed by him. I always felt that some of my classmates judging me and him. I still would always say hi to him. **"**

NATALIE
Sibling's condition: Hunter syndrome

" I wish that sometimes my sister would be able to control her fits of pain and not cry about them, although that is her only form of communication. Although I love her to bits, it is just hard. **"**

NOVELLE
Sibling's condition: Cerebral palsy

" In the first 15 years of my life, I had repeated vacations with limited activity. Airports weren't feasible and long road trips were a hassle. I don't mean to discredit the trips that I did have; I generally enjoyed myself and when I didn't, I found ways to occupy myself. But there was always some part of me that wished we were a "vacation" family, even though I knew it wasn't possible with my brother. I knew that more vacations would come eventually — when my brother passed away, though we never explicitly said that — but that didn't get rid of how I felt in the moment.

Instead, the only trips our full family could go on were our annual pilgrimages to San Antonio — 3 hours scrunched in the backseat of a minivan alongside luggage and medical supplies. These trips all blend together in my mind. It's the humming of *Shrek* on repeat, wandering the aisles of Buc-ee's for the best snacks to stock the van, and sitting in the resort lobby playing chess as snippets of my mother arguing with the front desk filtered in: "Yes, we requested a first-floor room" and "his wheelchair can't go up the stairs."

And then we'd be in the room. Always a slightly different location, but the same layout: a combined kitchen and living room and two bedrooms, each with their own bathroom. My sister and I always shared a room while my brother stayed with our parents, even though there was a pull-out couch meant for the third kid. He couldn't be alone. The first years, we brought a blow-up mattress. Eventually, the hotel got trundles that my parents could squeeze in a corner of their room by rearranging the furniture. Our last year at the hotel, we rented a hospital bed to be delivered to the hotel for my brother's use during our stay.

The year before we began our annual ventures to San Antonio we went to Great Wolf Lodge, where all three of us kids ran free, dazzled by the indoor waterpark and magic treasure hunt. I dreamed of many new adventures at many new places.

But that was an unsustainable dream; we needed someplace close that we could always count on to work for my brother. This new hotel would suit us better in the long run.

The beds weren't the only thing that changed over the years. The trips were like a bell curve. They got better, then they got worse. Over time, we learned the ins-and-outs of the hotel. We went to movie nights on the grass followed by s'mores, discovered our go-to meals at the built-in restaurant, and won the annual sand-castle building contest by the lazy river.

For a while, it was fun. But as my brother declined, we entered a period where my sister and I found ourselves alone. We couldn't do family activities; my brother was bound to his room. Even when we hired caretakers to watch him, my parents had to be ready to sprint to the room at any given moment.

I guess there were some positives to this. My sister and I were getting the freedoms that we so desperately desired at that age. It became too hard to wheel my brother to the restaurant just so he could eat a homemade pureed lunch — so I went by myself and felt like an adult when I said, "You can add it to my room charge." As we got older, my sister and I would discover the ins and outs of the hotel, making up our own ways to have fun.

Eventually though, we would drive back home, the vacation would come to a close, and school would begin again, bringing with it discussions and writing assignments of activities during the break. My classmates would fight over who did the best thing, proudly sharing their stories of driving across the country, camping under the stars, swimming at distant beaches, and skiing down steep peaks. I would stay quiet, reluctant to say that the most exciting thing I did was beat my dad in chess in the hotel lobby.

Now, the "eventually" has come. I can finally go on all the adventures that I so craved before, but all I want now is to go back to San Antonio with my brother. 🟥🟥

NICOLE
Sibling's condition: Hunter syndrome

🟥🟥 Growing up, I always watched my best friend wrestle and fight with his older brother. I remember one day coming home and asking my mom, "Why don't Charles and I wrestle or fight like that?" That was around the time that I started to realize that my older brother and I had a lot of differences. Charles was diagnosed with autism spectrum disorder at a young age after noticing some delayed development and aberrant social behaviors. Despite this, Charles still loved to play. In fact, around the time that I was a newborn, he loved carrying around a baby doll, just like my parents did with me. He was learning to read and write like his peers, and my parents had high hopes for the course of his development.

When Charles was seven years old, he had his first seizure, a grand mal seizure that lasted over twenty minutes. I remember feeling confused. At the age of five, I didn't know what was happening, nor did I grasp the severity of his situation. A few months later, he had another big seizure. My confusion turned to fear and a sense of helplessness. As Charles grew, his seizures became more frequent and intense. There were days when he had thousands of seizures back-to-back, spending months in the hospital where his team of doctors tried everything in their arsenal to control them. Charles often needed a wheelchair or a helmet with a face mask to protect him from the brutal consequences of his drop-seizures: busted lips and repeated concussions. My family desperately wanted answers. Why was this happening to Charles? What can we do to help him? A new form of genetic testing remarkably answered some of those questions. Charles was among the first patients to be diagnosed with a rare genetic disorder, Phelan-McDermid Syndrome, which was understood to be the cause of his neurodevelopmental phenotype and severe, treatment-resistant epilepsy. We were able to connect to other families facing similar challenges and suddenly had a sense of direction. However, it became apparent that this rare disorder had no cure or treatment. Charles' epilepsy continued to worsen, causing him to rapidly regress as he lost the verbal, motor, and cognitive skills he had fought so hard to learn through physical, occupational, and speech therapies.

Charles' complex health challenges brought hardship to every facet of our family's life. His unpredictable health meant I often had to take care of myself when my parents couldn't. I frequently felt resentment and embarrassment about my brother's differences. In public, people would point, laugh, and stare. There were times I wanted to distance myself from him, but there were also times when I wanted to hold him tight, to protect him. Fast-forward to today, at twenty-three years old, Charles is still battling seizures nearly every day and night. He's lost all of his verbal communication. Regardless, he is still the same adventurous, high-spirited, and kind brother that I have always known.

Despite his struggles, Charles has had a positive impact on the lives of so many. His unmatched resilience inspires me when I am faced with hardships of my own. My brother's struggles taught us that often the things we can't change, change us. Our family has become advocates, caregivers, educators, therapists, and lobbyists. Charles has been my primary motive for pursuing medicine and part of what inspired my passion for science. Every sibling has their own unique story, but I am confident that we all have an understanding and love for our siblings that many can't understand. "

NATHAN

Sibling's condition: Phelan-McDermid syndrome

SORROW

Introduction to Sorrow

Sorrow comes in many forms. Initially, this section was going to be titled "Grief" based on the experience of our brother passing away. Many of the stories and quotes below focus on grief that comes from a similar tragedy. But we realized that grief is only one form of sorrow and that other siblings of people with disabilities expressed other facets of sorrow, so we settled on sorrow.

Whatever form your sibling's disability takes, you may experience sorrow — sorrow over the many opportunities in life you and your sibling may never experience, sorrow at having to explain your sibling's disability, and sorrow again if people don't fully understand the disability.

Sorrow often accompanies many of the emotions of feeling isolated, different, or embarrassed.

In this section, we look at siblings of someone who has a disability who have felt sorrow. Hopefully, the experiences of other siblings in this section can offer ways to deal with sorrow. If nothing else, we hope that reading these experiences will let you know you aren't alone in feeling sorrow and there is a large community out there that can relate.

.

Quotes, Advice, and Stories

❝ I wish that my brother could just be free from what he goes through, and he too could have friends that he can meet regularly and talk to like how I do. ❞

DIYA
Sibling's condition: Autism

❝ I loved my brother, but sometimes I wished that I had the normal older sibling who could look out for me and give me advice. My friends have older siblings who gave them tips for high school and helped them with their homework. I never got that guidance. It's hard to see my friends with older siblings in college and know that's where my brother should — but never will — be. An older sibling normally protects the younger, but I always had to be the one protecting him. ❞

NATALIE
Sibling's condition: Hunter Syndrome

❝ Sometimes I don't want to be my brother's advocate. Sometimes I hate him so much it makes me cry at night…, and it makes me sad. Sometimes I want to shield my brother away when my friends come over. ❞

BLYTHE
Sibling's condition: Autism

When my brother first passed away, I knew that it would be really hard at first. I didn't expect for it to be an ongoing struggle where I continue to miss him daily, even two years later. Some days are harder than others — especially the holidays, which I associate so strongly with him. Holidays are meant to be happy days; because of my happy memories of him, they always have a sad tinge to them. Grief isn't a linear process, and there will always be ups and downs.

NATALIE
Sibling's condition: Hunter syndrome

It's hard to watch my brother not be able to interact with people much, and it's hard that I get to meet my friends, but he doesn't get to. So, each time my friends come over, I introduce them to him.

DIYA
Sibling's condition: Autism

Not knowing my parents' plan for my sister's long-term care, after they pass and if she is still alive, haunts me. I love her and would do anything for her, but she needs 24/7 care, and I need to have my own life and family and job, and if they leave her under my care and don't have a plan for the long term, I am afraid I will have to make the decision to either put my job and family aside or be responsible for finding a suitable group or nursing home for her to live in. I don't want to have to make that decision. I want my parents to figure that out, but I know they are too afraid to start looking at long term care plans.

EMMA
Sibling's condition: Dravet Syndrome

❝ Seeing people give my sister weird looks makes me sad. Knowing my sister will never have a great quality of life makes me feel bad. Having a sister with special needs makes my life 100 times harder than everyone else's and no one will ever know. I just wish my sister was normal and I could know her as a sister and live a normal life with her. ❞

SAMANTHA
Sibling's condition: Dravet syndrome

❝ Even with the continued grief, I can smile with joy knowing that I got to be present and love and be loved by my mother and it's something my sibling and I connect on. Throughout my time in graduate school as a dual family caregiver, I had the privilege of bringing my sib on campus to sit in with my classes, and along with our mom, attend fun dinner parties and research trips around the country. Of course, having time to myself has been valuable but I realized from the experience of our mother passing away that memories with loved ones are worth so much. ❞

VICTORIA
Sibling's condition: Intellectual/developmental disability

❝ In second grade my family went to Disney World with Make-A-Wish and stayed in a little village of dying kids. A group of teenage girls volunteered to paint our nails at La-Ti-Da Spa in the Castle of Miracles so they could embellish their graduation robes with blue and white community service cords. They talked about their plans for college: taking a year off for a mission trip, borrowing money from estranged parents to pay for New York, heading to junior college with plans to transfer. Maybe they didn't consider most of the kids whose delicate nails they filed and painted with bedazzled jewels wouldn't make it to college. Maybe they didn't want to.

With Make-A-Wish, fast passes cut us to the front of lines. People stared as my brother rolled by. Others watched out of the corners of their eyes instead. The question hung heavy: *What was wrong?* When I looked at him, I asked the same question. I asked how the heat of the park made him feel; I asked what he thought of the trip. I asked myself how he always felt. But he couldn't answer.

First park, first ride: A Cat in the Hat roller coaster in Seuss Landing. Years before, the movie had clawed white scars in my memory: a grown man clad in fur, whiskers jutting from weathered cheeks, purple jelly smeared across the children's furniture.

It took five minutes for my parents and the ride operator to strap my brother into the chair, ensuring the nylon straps weren't so loose he would slam against the back and weren't so tight that it squeezed his skin red. Three sharp buzzes sounded, and the lights dimmed, and the cart bumped along its track. Within moments, that morning's sickeningly sweet cotton candy rose in my throat, and I threw up in my mouth. I felt gnarled fingers knotting intestines, cold sweat trickling through warm air on goosebumped skin, and black spots of vertigo seeping through vision. Between turns and hills, my parents whispered of motion sickness and medicine, and I thought of the scene when the kids rode their unconscious nanny like a cart through their deformed house of bent chairs on walls and fires blooming out of suspended toilets. At least they didn't vomit.

For the rest of the trip, I held my brother's hand, skipped the lines, and stepped aside as we got to the front of the rides, feeling breakfast rising. My brother only went on the tame rides, so we sat together and waited, and I wondered if the same motion sickness grabbed him.

• • •

The first time a seizure stole my brother, we called the ambulance and prayed. I cried at first because my parents did and I felt I should, and then I couldn't stop the tears, even when the other's eyes dried. In my head, I scripted a list of goodbyes, but I didn't know the proper pattern of words, and the list was too short and too shallow — I could tell him I loved him and I'd miss him, but I couldn't capture it. It was incomplete. It wasn't right.

Research suggests that motion sickness and partial seizures may be triggered by the same electric waves from the brain. Motion sickness is a typical ailment: sensory overload, sudden nausea, spinning room, but you recover, move on, nothing more than a blip. Seizure effects linger. Thoughts fuzz and become beads on a bracelet growing harder and harder to string. Headaches tear through your temples. Sleep summons, but when you close your eyes, you can't.

By his final year, seizures were a standard of his life. His breath caught, his body fell rigid, and we counted the seconds trickling into minutes until time resumed for him, but I feared one day his clock would stop too long. I wish he hadn't been robbed of speech by then. I wish I could have told him that I too felt suspended in that constant state of motion sickness, of electric waves from the brain. I wish I could have told him all we had in common.

• • •

When I was younger, I dreamed of exploring the universe. I would be the first contact with alien life, bringing them under human control; I would be the first step onto Martian dust, claiming the planet for America, claiming it as a natural extension of mankind and all the other rhetoric I inhaled.

60% to 80% of space travelers experience motion sickness. Before promethazine was introduced, the incapacitating nausea led to a 10% reduction in efficiency.

Now, my childhood vision of exploration rings of historical colonization and cruel subjugation. Now, I know I would vomit on the take-off. Now, I'm more content to watch the stars from afar and craft my own constellations without swimming through the silver liquid streams.

Except sometimes I want to feel my brother's seizures. I want my senses overloaded. I want to feel motion sick. I can't board a rocket, and so, I run.

I run until I lose my own body, until I am lost like him, until my head spins and I wonder if on the next step, my foot won't hit pavement, and I'll float away like that flying house from *Up* and my heart could be the old man inside. Most days, I run on an empty stomach. (*Why?* To help with cramps; I have no appetite; I want to be skinnier. *I don't know.*) It makes me dizzy. I do it anyway.

In a block, my breathing hastens (in half if I forget my inhalers); in a mile, my legs burn, but I keep running. Plastic shoes melt on frying-pan pavement in Southern Summers, shin splints spike down the sides of my calves, and I pass by the same group of middle school girls in Lululemon that judge my old shirts and shorts, but if I'm dizzy enough, I notice nothing.

My family wasn't built for running. My mom collects injuries like trophies as proof of her former hard work: plantar fasciitis, strained hamstring, aching back. My dad walks marathons in miles to 80s music and history podcasts but never picks up the pace. For my brother, walking was a rarity turned impossibility with age. When I run, I feel I need to down extra miles like a jug of soda until I feel sick to compensate for the rest of my family.

I run until my vision blurs, until I cannot make out the lyrics of whatever break-up Taylor Swift is lamenting this time in my headphones, until I forget what street I'm on and can't decipher the sign anyway.

Then I run a little more until I feel truly motion sick, and I sit down and stretch — pull and tug at muscles to loosen them — and I wonder what it would feel to cut my muscles right in half until I couldn't move at all. Until I too was bound in a wheelchair.

• • •

The sensory conflict theory explains motion sickness as when the body's three main sensory inputs send mixed signals the brain cannot handle. When I think of my brother, I still feel the mixed signals. The world, the ashes, the funeral, the eulogy all proclaim he is lost. But he cannot be because how does a star blink out of existence? No—he was meant to shine and last longer, even if doctors said he wasn't. They said he was lucky to make it to seventeen.

We have four Netflix profiles under our account: my parents', my sister's, mine, and his. Two years and no one has used his. Once a week, I click on his profile to see the Continue Watching bar, forever locked between scenes of *Shrek*, the red never to gain another pixel on the remaining grey bar. I see the recommended movies: all that the algorithm thinks he would enjoy but won't be able to verify.

We still call it his room. Not the guest room it has been repurposed as, not the game room we almost made it: *Jake's room*. Is it worse to call it Jake's room like he is still here, or to pretend it's any other room like he never was?

Whenever I think of him, it takes a moment to switch to past tense. In English, I reflexively say *Jake is* and have to correct myself to *Jake was*. In Spanish, when I deliberately consider the translation of every word, it's easier to remember: *Mi hermano era*. And when my teacher corrects it to *Mi hermano es*, I let him. The transition between tenses is bumpy, and I feel the gnarled fingers knotting intestines, cold sweat trickling through warm air on goosebumped skin, and black spots of vertigo seeping through vision. I feel the electric waves from my brain and I feel his seizures and I feel like him. I am back in Seuss Landing, but this time, I cannot hold his hand and avoid the line. "

NATALIE

Sibling's condition: Hunter syndrome

I don't know when I realized my brother was going to die; there's no distinct memory of my parents sitting me down with fake smiles and teary eyes. But, it wasn't something I was consciously aware of my whole life. Somewhere along the way, I understood this without being told, largely due to three things: the crises, the gradual decline, and the extraneous information.

The crises were sporadic and inconsistent, ranging in severity and time. It was his first seizure, and though the details are muddled, a clear image sticks with me: my mom cradling him on the floor of our foyer against the sounds of ambulances coming from the station a block away, their red lights glaring against the night windows. The word "first" is important, as seizures became constant afflictions; by the end, he seemed to be having a seizure more days than not.

Then there was the gradual decline, where everything slowly got worse. He went from running to walking to standing to a wheelchair to confined to a hospital bed at the house. The weekly infusions shifted from the hospital to our home, and Hospice joined our household. Instead of chewing, he had mushed foods. A tube ran up his nose to help him breathe. His infectious smile and joyous laughter became less and less common, and we wondered what he still understood.

Finally, there was the extraneous information: things my parents didn't tell me directly, but were bubbling in the background. It was when I finally learned the medical name for his condition — Mucopolysaccharidosis II, not just Hunter syndrome — and could appease my Googling tendencies to find the WebMD page: "Unlikely to reach adulthood." It was when I came downstairs to my mom on the couch, saving photos of my brother to a folder on her computer "to prepare." (These photos would come in handy; she was just a few years early.) It was my dad telling my sister and me that we needed to be careful, staying out of our brother's room when we had a runny nose or cough, because he "probably won't make it" if he got sick. It was when people my parents hadn't spoken to in years sent us meals and flowers with cards full of condolences in the final days.

Those moments were the worst, because it was the world confirming what was visible to me in other ways. If everything said he was going to die, there was no way to avoid that reality.

Even though all these signs were pointing to the inevitable curtain closing, it was still a surprise. As they say, everyone is immortal until proven otherwise. We all knew it was coming, but it had been coming for years — and every other time things got tough, he pulled through.

But I don't focus on those things. I remember him at his happiest. Going to Disney World when he met his heroes: Buzz Lightyear and Woody. Laying squished next to him in his bed, watching Max and Ruby — my favorite of his TV shows. The house ever busy, a comfortable hum of his movie, his nurse, and the medical machinery in his room.

But the good and the bad are so intertwined. We were in Disney World because it was his Make-A-Wish. His bed was a hospital bed and he was 16 watching children's cartoons. The house was busy because he couldn't be alone and he needed constant care.

Still, though, there is happiness in every memory because he was there. 🙶

NICOLE
Sibling's condition: Hunter syndrome

🙶 I was seventeen when my dad passed away and he was forty-six. Seven of us siblings were still living at home, including my three brothers on the Autism Spectrum. My mom soldiered on for twenty-five years as a single parent until she passed away at sixty-eight. My brothers were all living with my mom when she passed away. Mom had not included us in future planning and would not consider putting our brothers on a waiting list to live in group homes or any setting away from the family home. My older sister and I were devastated by the loss of our mother, but we did not have the luxury of spending time on our own grief. We had to become the primary caregivers and advocates for our brothers.

Losing parents is always hard, but adding on a huge new responsibility makes the situation so much worse. I would encourage siblings and parents to do some serious future planning, and it is not just trusts and waiting lists that would help. A letter of intent or at least a detailed file with important information would be helpful. Future planning should be a team effort that includes the sibling with a disability. Even if parents are not willing to include their children in future planning, there are ways siblings can prepare on their own. My sister and I wish we had educated ourselves in advance rather than waiting for the time we knew would come. I recommend the book *The Sibling Survival Guide* to all siblings; it is what I wish had when my last parent passed away.

In addition to the loss of my parents, I have also lost three of my siblings, my younger two brothers Patrick and Michael who were on the Autism Spectrum, and my typical sister Mary. All of these losses were sudden and unexpected and occurred in the last three years. The most recent loss of my sister was less than six months ago. My remaining siblings and I are still reeling from these losses and feel that we had not processed one before the next one occurred.

I lost my brother Patrick three years ago, the day before my birthday and a week before Christmas. He was living happily in an apartment building where all the tenants were people with intellectual disabilities that provided support and guidance as needed. He loved living there and had many friends and a job as a bagger at a grocery store. He had a terrible fall that took his life and shocked his family and community.

Patrick loved the holidays and brought joy to everyone with the way he embraced everything Christmas. Some of his community made our family bracelets that say *Live Like Patrick* because he never met a person whom he did not think was beautiful. Patrick was a master of flattery; he loved to compliment people. I miss being his beautiful sister.

Michael passed away a year and half ago. In addition to his Autism, he had schizoaffective disorder. His mental illness required a cocktail of heavy psych drugs. Those meds wreaked havoc on his body, but he needed them to stay stable. Michael suffered from visual and auditory hallucinations, but he was the sweetest man and the beloved baby of the family. As siblings, we felt protective of all of our brothers but especially Michael. His death, less a year after Patrick's, was profoundly painful for us.

Our typical sister Mary was our most recent loss. Mary was the keeper of family tradition and replicated our mother's Christmas Eve party. Our brothers very much looked forward to it and enjoyed the big party as did we all. We have a large extended family, and they were all welcome. At our largest, I think there were fifty people. Mary had no warning symptoms and died in her sleep: she was only fifty-nine. As we approach Christmas, her siblings dread this holiday. We will step up, but we know we can't fill her shoes.

As would be expected, all the siblings have dealt with this trifecta of loss in different and unique ways. I can't speak for my other sisters, but I felt these losses so profoundly that I felt physically ill enough to go to the doctor. The stress and grief gave me palpitations and chest pain. Due to our family history, twice I underwent testing to check out my heart. I felt better after results came out normal but it took a while for the symptoms to go away.

I personally found it helpful to turn to my fellow siblings both through S.I.B.S. (Supporting Illinois Brothers and Sisters), our Illinois chapter of The Sibling Leadership Network, and through SibNet on

Facebook. Between my own losses and those of other siblings that I know, we realized that there are very limited grief supports for ourselves and our siblings with disabilities. Last June there were two small breakout sessions on grief at the SLN conference. Each session was packed, and it was obvious that there is a need out there for this kind of support. It is a goal of both the SLN and S.I.B.S. to help fill this need. **"**

NORA
Sibling's condition: Autism

GRATEFUL

Introduction to Grateful

It is easy to focus only on the negatives. We choose to also focus on the positives. A common underlying theme we saw when gathering material for this book was siblings of someone with a disability choosing to be grateful even when sharing painful memories. We use the term "grateful" here, but it could often be replaced with love and appreciation.

At times, it can be difficult to be positive. But as many of the quotes and stories in previous sections have shown, you can still feel gratitude, love, and appreciation for your sibling and what they have taught you.

Having a sibling with a disability gives you a unique perspective on life, and that perspective can be beneficial. We know that personally: Our brother made us stronger, more empathetic, and more mature and strengthened our relationships with the rest of our family. We are thankful for every lesson that he taught us.

Acknowledging feeling grateful isn't to invalidate any negative feelings. But this book wouldn't be complete if we didn't mention the positives that people experience. We wanted to highlight that there is something to be grateful for in every situation.

Quotes, Advice, and Stories

❝ My brother Johnny is the brightest light in my life, and I cannot imagine having a better brother and best friend to grow up with. Johnny is the oldest of the triplets, with Maggie in the middle and me as the youngest. I try to tell Johnny that those were the best four minutes of his life as the first triplet, but I know how incredibly blessed I have been that Johnny has been in every second of my life. He has taught me so much about love, strength, patience, responsibility, and kindness. Johnny has provided me with so much laughter and joy, even through points in our lives that may have been more difficult. He has absolutely made me a better man, and I can't wait to continue to grow up together as we take on the world. ❞

VINCE
Sibling's condition: Autism

❝ Maybe it's because I'm younger than my brother with special needs, but I have always been accepting of him. I have always loved all of him and have never wished for anything less or anything more. As his sister, I not only have been able to appreciate every part of my brother, but I've also felt like every part of him will always be a small part of me. ❞

CLAIRE
Sibling's condition: Autism

❝ Trying to understand my brother gets me a step closer to becoming his best friend. ❞

LYDIA
Sibling's condition: Autism (PDD-NOS)

❝ Now, Susie and I have a unique sister relationship. I help her and she helps me. That is how all of Susie's volunteer work kind of got started. Everyone knows my job is busy and there are always a million things I want to get accomplished. Well, what if you had a mini assistant ... someone to make name tags, cut out crafts, stuff mailings and so on ... someone like, say a sister? When things started getting busy for me, I started bringing things home for Susie to help with. She was a great help but did it on her "own" time (meaning when she absolutely couldn't think of anything better to do). I was grateful for her help and decided what if I paid her for all the hours she volunteered. We sat down and she loved the idea. She asked for minimum wage. I asked her if she knew how much that was; she didn't. So I told her it was $8 an hour with the sister discount. She agreed but with one stipulation ... I must pay her in iTunes gift cards! Over the next few months, I brought home projects and she gave me invoices for how much I owed her. It was really adding up and she loved it. One day I said, "You spent 6 hours on cutting boardmaker pictures!!!" She said "Yep, you told me they had to be perfect." Months went by and Susie decided it was time for her to branch out and start volunteering outside of the home with many different organizations. She is exceptional. ❞

LIZ
Sibling's condition: Chromosome 2 disorder,
heart condition, visual and hearing impairment

66 My brother was born sick. His name is Conner; he is 12. He loved to dress up in costumes! He used to talk, he stopped when he was 8. He is very smart and makes people laugh. He used to play and have fun, now he can't do very much. Conner has to go to lots of doctors and has had lots of operations. When Conner could talk, he said I was his favorite person! For all of these reasons and more he will always be my favorite brother and hero! 99

JAMIE (younger)
Sibling's condition: Hunter syndrome

66 Take advantage of every moment with your sibling — the good and the bad—because there is always something to learn from every experience. 99

JAMIE
Sibling's condition: Hunter syndrome

66 I am fortunate to know and be known by my sibling who has been my best friend in life. Although we may not communicate in traditional ways, we get each other and fully accept each other. It's love. 99

VICTORIA
Sibling's condition: Intellectual/developmental disability

66 If you feel like your problems aren't big enough, they are. It's going to be hard, trust me, but you will be thankful. 99

BLYTHE
Sibling's condition: Autism

❝ Having a sibling with a disability was difficult, but he taught me so many lessons and has made me the person I am today. ❞

NATALIE
Sibling's condition: Hunter syndrome

❝ I have learned to value the time and experiences I get to have with my family, even when they're stressful and my impulse may be to withdraw. ❞

VICTORIA
Sibling's condition: Intellectual/Developmental Disability

❝ I have an autistic brother who is 12 years old, so we have a ten-year age difference. I believe that having someone with special needs in my family changed my perspective on the world; I'm more understanding. What other people take for granted, I take with gratitude. I notice the minor goals that others overlook. I believe it is difficult at first, but once I accepted it and understood his world a little better, I was able to see the beauty in the journey. My journey with him has played a big role in shaping me as a person. ❞

LYDIA
Sibling's condition: Autism

❝ Seeing my brother's daily hardships helps me put my own challenges into perspective. ❞

NATHAN
Sibling's condition: Phelan-McDermid syndrome

❝ Summing up my sibling life: I spent some time at Ronald McDonald House growing up while she had a lot of surgeries; I knew how to call 911 and report her oxygen levels by the time I was 4; I realized very young that every time I got sick I had to go stay at my grandparents; I got suspended from high school the one year we overlapped for fighting; I put a ton of pressure on myself to do well in everything (in theory, one less thing for my family to worry about, or so I thought), and yet my parents will tell you I was much harder to raise. I believe I am a better person because of my sibling. ❞

LIZ
Sibling's condition: Chromosome 2 disorder,
heart condition, visual and hearing impairment

❝ Vacations are hard. It's always about where's Eli, what's Eli doing, and have we told everyone in this hotel about Eli. It has always been hard, and especially as I have gotten older, I have had a bigger responsibility for Eli. I used to hate it because vacation was when it was time for me to relax. A time for me to forget. I used to get so mad at my parents for making me watch Eli the whole day. But now, I've learned to enjoy it. Eli and I have gotten closer and bonded in an unconventional way, talking about what is obsessing his mind and things he has done today. I am thankful for the time I spend with Eli. It makes me a better person. It makes me grow and learn to love Eli. ❞

BLYTHE
Sibling's condition: Autism

❝ Have you ever wondered what it is like to have a sibling with a disorder? Well you have come to the right place because my brother is autistic. Surprisingly, it is not that bad. It is actually pretty good. I barely have any arguments with my brother. But of course, everything has a downside. Every day I have to clean up after him, and sometimes he can make a huge mess and when I say huge, I mean it. Gets pretty tiring at times but I always manage to work through it. 🟉🟉

JONAS
Sibling's condition: Autism

🟉🟉 Patience is the first step, and communicating among family creates unconditional love that is hard to put into words. 🟉🟉

LYDIA
Sibling's condition: Autism (PDD-NOS)

🟉🟉 You will see people for who they are and how beautiful they can be. 🟉🟉

LIZ
Sibling's condition: Chromosome 2 disorder,
heart condition, visual and hearing impairment

🟉🟉 Growing up, I dreamed of meeting someone my age who had a sibling with a disability who could understand the roller coaster of life at home. You would think the population of San Diego could easily meet this request, but no one showed up in our circle. My brother is 5 years younger than I am and has Cerebral Palsy. He cannot do anything independently and requires 24-hour care. He does not communicate in the traditional sense of using words; however, our family understands him most of the time through eye movements, body movements, face scrunches, vocalizations, cries, laughter, and smiles. His smile is one of the most beautiful things about him.

Over the years, my brother has had over 18 surgeries, 16 rounds of pneumonia, and multiple emergency room trips and ambulance rides. I don't think there is anything this kid can't survive, and it amazes me how he is so incredibly strong, yet fragile, at the same time. When I was a child, I knew I would do anything to protect my brother from anyone or anything, yet simultaneously, I wished to be part of another family so I could experience "normal" and not have to be his protector. I think that is what having a sibling with a disability is: you find so many opposing ideas and feelings to be true in the same moment.

When I applied to colleges, I only applied out-of-state. I wanted to be as far from home as possible. But within a couple of months of my adventure, a surgery left my brother in the ICU again. I felt guilty to be away, and then relieved I didn't have to spend my days in the hospital supporting my mom, and then guilty for feeling relieved. Shortly after this event, my brother moved out of our home and into a live-in facility. I was angry and upset that my parents allowed him to leave home. I did not understand their need for help because I saw myself as a third parent, which was far from my role. The emotional lines were blurred for me in my sibling role because so early on I was forced to be more independent, to learn empathy for others, to sort out my emotional needs at convenient times for my parents, and to "grow up" sooner than I was ready. This is not to the fault of anyone but circumstance, and many siblings would probably agree.

After my brother moved into his facility, I went to visit during spring break. I did not like a lot about the facility except for two things: He was surrounded by people like him, and he had a recreation therapist who made the facility more of a home. After that visit, I transferred schools, states, and majors to do something I was newly intrigued by. My drive came from acceptance and understanding of the role I have played since I was 5. That caring for others, giving people a voice, and creating fun for populations at risk was something I was good at and motivated to do for others. So, although I thought I wanted to run away from the roller coaster of what came with being a sibling, instead I found my passion and strength from being a sibling. And after over a decade of working with kids, teens, and adults with a variety of disabilities and mental health diagnoses, I can confidently say that I have accepted who I am and where I came from, and that I owe it to my brother to be in a role where I can help others. "

JESSICA
Sibling's condition: Cerebral palsy

" I don't like change. I hate it really — I like my plans and my firm schedules, and whenever something deviates, my reflex is to try to mold it back to the original plan. When my friends cancel something at the last minute, I feel a tightness in my chest at the change. But even though I don't like it, I know how to deal with change.

Growing up with a sibling with a disability is growing up around change and uncertainty. Many days I had to cancel plans because my brother had a last-minute medical emergency, and my parents couldn't give me a ride. Other times my parents and I would be planning to go out to dinner, my brother's caregiver would cancel, and we had to stay at home instead. It was never intentional and there was no one to blame, but still it was still hard and frustrating. Some of the changes were small and some were large, but they always disrupted the rhythm I tried to build in my life. But because I never had a choice and had to deal with the situation anyway, I learned how to deal with it.

In some cases like mine, growing up with a sibling with a disability is also growing up around loss. As my brother's condition progressed, his skills regressed. It was difficult to watch someone I loved so much struggle for so long. In 2019, I lost my brother when he succumbed to his disease. I continue to deal with that loss every day.

In 2020, the pandemic changed the entire world. I saw people who were used to following their perfect schedules struggling to adapt to the uncertainty: they never had to deal with a situation like that before. But I knew how to deal with the shift and navigate unfamiliar waters. While others were drowning in the uncertainty, I knew how to stay afloat. Like most people, I've faced a lot of change since March 2020. My day-to-day life was changed. My interactions with friends were changed. School was changed; sports were changed. The change bothered me and is still difficult, but I know how to accept it.

During the pandemic, I also lost a lot. I lost connections with friends. I lost passions for things I used to love, and I lost the ability to access many more of my passions as I was trapped inside my house. Like dealing with the change, dealing with the loss was difficult but familiar. No matter what I lost and continue to lose because of the pandemic, I know that I can survive it because I have lost much worse. If I can survive losing my brother, I can survive whatever else the world and COVID takes away and I can survive whatever other challenges the future brings. It doesn't mean these other challenges aren't hard, frustrating, and sad, but I know that the feelings will eventually fade, and things will get better again.

Growing up with a brother with a disability was challenging, and I continue to deal with some of the difficulties, but it prepared me for life. I am forever grateful for that.**"**

NATALIE
Sibling's condition: Hunter syndrome

When Vinayak was born, I was probably the happiest person in the world. He completed our family; he took our happiness to an all-new level. What hit us really hard was that he was diagnosed with autism when he was 2 and a half years old. We initially misunderstood it as a hearing disability, but it was clear later on. Vinayak and I had a very different relationship albeit the strongest one you can ever imagine. Society always looked at him with pity in their eyes. What they don't see is the smile plastered on his face, his strong personality, and his mind sharper than many "normal" people. People ask me how will he adjust to the world? They will feel defeated when my little brother can do so many things they can't. He can solve a 100+ pieces puzzle within 3 minutes; he is a baking master. To top it all, he won a gold medal for sports at school. Just when Vinayak and I were leading a normal life, we lost our father four years ago, when he was 15 years old. During this time, he showed so much endurance, stability, and maturity. He kept us strong through those times, far beyond what a "normal" person can do. He performed all the rituals with a smile on his face, and he expressed emotions in his own beautiful way.

He recently passed his 10th grade, another achievement to all his others. Plus I can see some fashionista vibes in my little teenager man. He does not suffer from autism, but he will suffer from the way you treat him. Hence, I try to create as much awareness on autism that can help autism acceptance. He is different, not less. He has taught me more about life than anyone else in the world ever will. As the saying goes, hope is a rope that will swing you through life. I don't know what the future holds, but with him in my life, I will be just fine!!

Behind every autistic child is a family that stood by him/her rock solid. "Why fit in when you were born to stand out" —Dr. Seuss. 🟢

SUVI
Sibling's condition: Autism

Resources

Organizations

These are organizations we have found helpful. Descriptions are based on the "About" pages of the following websites. If you are involved with an organization that supports siblings of people with disabilities, please contact us at contact@specialsiblingsconnect.org to be added to our list of resources on our website (www.specialsiblingsconnect.org/resources).

AKALAKA
www.akalaka.org

AKALAKA helps serve disability and care communities. Among other things, they provide people who care for their siblings with education, resources, and other support.

Sibling Leadership Network
siblingleadership.org

Sibling Leadership Network works to connect siblings with social, emotional, governmental, and provisional support.

Sibling Support Project
siblingsupport.org

Sibling Support Project works to support brothers and sisters of people with special developmental, health, and mental health needs. Their initiatives include Sibshops, online communities for brothers and sisters, publications, workshops, and training.

Siblings with a Mission

www.siblingswithamission.org

Siblings with a Mission is dedicated to supporting and empowering siblings of individuals with special needs. They do this by providing siblings and family members an opportunity to share stories, make suggestions, and make friends. Their resources include story columns, resource databases, monitored video conversations, webchat forums, sibling workshops, and family conferences.

Special Needs Siblings

specialneedssiblings.com

Special Needs Siblings, provides families with disabled individuals education, resources, and supportive programs to educate, empower, and encourage siblings.

Books

These are books we have found helpful. If you wrote a book for siblings of people with disabilities or found a book useful, please contact us at contact@specialsiblingsconnect.org to request that we add your book to the list of books on our website (www.specialsiblingsconnect.org/resources).

Billy's Sister: Life when your sibling has a disability
by Jessica Leving

Combining the author's personal experience with the support of licensed clinical social workers, *Billy's Sister* explores the good and the bad when growing up with a sibling who has a disability.

Emotions of a Super Sibling
by Tamara Cullere

Emotions of a Super Sibling explores the range of emotions that a supersibling — someone with a sibling who is different or has a rare disease — may experience.

I Have Needs Too!:
Supporting the child whose sibling has special needs
by Elizabeth A. Batson

Using experiences from siblings of kids with special needs and the author herself, *I Have Needs Too!* offers advice for parents to help understand and support their kids through different issues and emotions.

Special Siblings: Growing Up with
Someone with a Disability
by Mary McHugh

Special Siblings shares Mary McHugh's personal story, supplemented with research and interviews of over 100 other siblings, to explore a range of emotions and help readers understand issues that siblings sometimes face.

You Are a Superhero, Too!
by Brittnie Blackburn

Written from a parent's point-of-view, *You Are a Superhero, Too!* acknowledges the unique dynamics that accompany living with a person with a disability. At the same time, it highlights a sibling's essential role, showing they are not less loved or important.

Views from Our Shoes: Growing Up with
a Brother or Sister with Special Needs
by Donald Meyer

View From Our Shoes shares the experiences of 45 kids of siblings with a disability of varying ages and conditions.

Acknowledgments

Thank you to all the organizations that helped spread the word about our project and encouraged siblings to submit stories to us. This book wouldn't be possible without these organizations. Thanks especially to:

AKALAKA

American Cleft Palate-Craniofacial Association

A-One

MPS Society

Northwest Special Recreation Association

PM Pals

Sandy Feet Initiative

Sibling Support Project

Sibshop chapters

Supporting Illinois Brothers and Sisters

We would also like to thank every sibling who contributed. Every quote and story matters, and your words have the potential to impact so many. It can be scary to be vulnerable and share your story. We appreciate you trusting your stories with us.

A final thanks to those who reviewed our book and supported us:

Bevin Shields Barrett, M.Ed, LPC

Dacia Napier, MD, our brother's godmother

Krista Formica, MD, pediatrician

Nathalie English, MD

Our Parents

Want to support Special Siblings Connect?

If you enjoyed *By Siblings, For Siblings* and want to donate copies to other siblings, go to Special Sibling Connect's website (specialsiblingsconnect.org/book).
For every $10 donated, one book can be donated.

If you want to help us grow our social media presence to reach more people, follow and share us on all platforms at @specialsiblingsconnect.

If you want to share your own story as a sibling, go to our website specialsiblingsconnect.org/join.
Any questions, comments, or concerns?
Email contact@specialsiblingsconnect.org